Quality Assur
Continuing Education Programmes:

A Handbook for HEIs

Published by Quality Promotion Unit, University College Cork, Ireland, on behalf of the QACEP Project

© Quality Promotion Unit, UCC, 2011

Design:
Sarah Slattery
slattery.sarahm@gmail.com

Printing:
Hackett's Printers, Cork
1st edition

ISBN: 978-1-906642-39-6

Date: September 2011

Foreword

This handbook outlines the principal outcomes and results of the activities carried out from October 2009 to September 2011 within the European project "Quality Assurance for Higher Education Institutions' Continuing Education Programmes" (www.qacep.eu).

First contacts among the eight institutions partnered in the QACEP consortium started in September 2008. Following the brainstorming stage, the six universities and the two associations involved shared the existing reflections and the common interest in a better understanding for the need for appropriate quality assurance for continuing education programmes in their own institutions and in the national context, through comparison with other European Higher Education Institutions. Moreover the common interest in finding solutions and tools to review and ameliorate the procedures raised different kind of questions, including *what are the features of continuing education programmes relevant for defining suitable QA approaches and tools, compared to Bachelor-Master-Doctorate programmes?; how to get learners' opinions to facilitate review of the project, including consideration of specific issues for learners and of the learning objectives?; how to articulate a proper self-evaluation activity?; what kind of role is there for external stakeholders?.*

The project facilitated the direct participation, both in the Core Group Workshops organised by the Consortium and in the activities developed in each institution, of more than 60 people: staff responsible for Quality Assurance and Continuing Education, Continuing Education Programme managers and coordinators, teachers/academics, members of governing bodies, and also staff expert in surveys and ICT innovation in Higher Education Institutions.

This Handbook provides an important support for the dissemination of the outcomes of the Project and its purpose is to encourage the consideration of issues in determining quality assurance of Higher Education Institutions' Continuing Education Programmes that could lead to many possible directions, at different levels and with different objectives. For example: wider comparative analysis on continuing education and specific Quality Assurance practices; testing, implementation, and further customization of the tools developed.

Dr. Carla Salvaterra, Vice Rector for International Relations, University of Bologna
Angela Ribeiro Cavazzuti, Quality Assurance Unit, University of Bologna

Contents

Acknowledgements 6

Acronyms Used 7

Chapter 1: **Introduction and Description of project** 9

Chapter 2: **The QACEP Framework** 21

Chapter 3: **Step 1: Planning and Design of CEP** 31

Chapter 4: **Step 2: Implementation and Delivery of CEP** 37

Chapter 5: **Step 3: Monitoring of CEP** 43

Chapter 6: **Step 4: Continuous Quality Improvement of CEP** 47

Chapter 7: **Looking to the future** 51

Appendices:

A. QACEP Comparative Analysis Template 55

B. QACEP Evaluation Report for Continuing Education Programmes 67

C. QACEP Student Evaluation Questionnaire (CEP Leavers Questionnaire) 78

D. QACEP Consortium Partner Profiles 83

Bibliography **86**

Acknowledgements

The QACEP Project Consortium partners wish to acknowledge the funding received from the European Commission under the Lifelong Learning Programme - Erasmus - Modernisation of Higher Education (project number 502370-LLP-1-2009-IT-ERASMUS-EMHE). The Consortium also wishes to acknowledge the contributions and participation of the programme managers and directors within the partner institutions who contributed so much at all stages of the project.

Acronyms Used

CE:	Continuing Education
CEP:	Continuing Education Programme
EC:	European Commission
EHEA:	European Higher Education Area
ESG:	Standards and Guidelines for Quality Assurance in the European Higher Education Area
EU:	European Union
EUA:	European University Association
HEI:	Higher Education Institution
ICT:	Information & Communications Technology
IL3-UB:	Institute for Lifelong Learning, University of Barcelona
NQF:	National Qualifications Framework
PDCA:	Planning, Doing, Checking, Acting
QA:	Quality Assurance
QACEP:	Quality Assurance of Continuing Education Programmes
SME:	Small and Medium Enterprises
SWOT:	Strengths, Weaknesses, Opportunities, Threats
UCC:	University College Cork
UW:	University of Warsaw
UNIBO:	University of Bologna

Chapter 1

Introduction and Description of Project

"The aim of education is to enable individuals to continue their education .... (and) the object and reward of learning is continued capacity for growth."

John Dewey

Context

Advanced knowledge-based societies require innovative and creative educational systems that are able to respond immediately to specific needs of the continuously evolving and changing labour market and of society in general; appropriate education and training of adults is required in order to prevent forms of generational discrimination in the employment policies and in society generally. In addition, well specialized and graduate professionals and their organisations are required to improve and update personal skills and competences on a regular basis, often as a pre-requisite for professional recognition. In this context, Higher Education Institutions (HEIs) play a fundamental role in providing research-based higher education and professional development services for lifelong learners, creating opportunities for retraining and/or advanced specialization for all. Furthermore HEIs have a responsibility to ensure transparency and quality in this learning experience.

Role of HEIs in Continuing Education Programmes

Efforts are still necessary for "a more systematic development of flexible learning paths to support lifelong learning" as well as "to increase the sharing of good practice and to work towards a common understanding of the role of higher education in lifelong learning"[1]. In pursuit of this aim, HEIs must define articulated strategies for lifelong learning not only by experimenting with specific tools and paths in degree programmes, but also by finding "ways to open up educational services to returning learners"[2]. In the last few years, different surveys, for example the EUA's "Trends"[3] reports and BeFlex[4] project, have analyzed learning practices in the European Higher Education Area (EHEA) and have provided evidence that one response HEIs actually give to social, cultural and economic challenges, in terms of lifelong learning needs, is the provision of continuing education and training courses addressed primarily to the post graduate level, but also applicable to secondary students with professional experience.

---

1 Cf. London Communiqué, 2007 and Leuven/Louvain-la-Neuve Communiqué, 2009
2 Cf. EUA, Charter on Lifelong Learning
3 www.eua.be/Publications.aspx
4 www.eucen.eu/BeFlex BeFlex Project Final Report

Why the QACEP Project?
The real relevance and importance of the increasing level of continuing education programme offerings highlight the need to include all the Continuing Education Programmes offered by HEIs in the quality assurance systems already in place and to develop appropriate approaches in order to ensure the continuous improvement of these programmes and guarantee their quality. An adapted approach for the quality assurance of CEPs is crucial in considering the specific objectives of these programmes, the specific target groups, the variety of stakeholders involved, and their relationship with the labour market and society. There is clear evidence of the need for creating and sharing practices and tools in this field, both within a national and also a transnational perspective.

This has been the background for the project "Quality Assurance for HEIs' Continuing Education Programmes"[5], a project funded with support from the European Commission (Lifelong Learning Programme – Erasmus – Modernisation of Higher Education). This two year project commenced in October 2009 and was conducted by a Consortium composed of eight institutions: six HEIs (Aalto University, Institute for Lifelong Learning of the University of Barcelona, Katholieke Universiteit Leuven, University College Cork, University of Bologna, University of Warsaw), and two associations representing a large number of other HEIs, the Inter-University Consortium AlmaLaurea and the Coimbra Group. A brief profile of each partner institution is provided in Appendix D.

The principal aim was to develop a general framework for quality assurance applicable to CEPs offered by HEIs, compatible with and adapted to the needs and specific context of each individual HEI, and to elaborate detailed and practical tools for the assessment of their quality.

Origin of Project

HEIs are key actors in promotion of lifelong learning. Increasingly they are being called on to increase and enhance their efforts in providing research-based higher

---

[5] QACEP: a project funded with support from the European Commission (Lifelong Learning Programme – Erasmus – Modernisation of Higher Education). http://www.qacep.eu

education for lifelong learners and in guaranteeing the quality of their learning provision. This is a key objective of the Bologna Process in the EHEA. A response HEIs give to social challenges in terms of lifelong learning need is the provision of advanced continuing education and training courses. Considering the increasing and significant relevance of this type of provision at the intersection between HEIs, professional practice and general vocational continuing education and training, the need for transparency and external accountability and for assessment and assurance of their quality, just as for higher education mainstream courses, is evident. The concept for the project was originally developed by the University of Bologna who became the coordinator of the project, together with the institutions partnered in the consortium.

Project Approach
The activities for the QACEP project were organised in three stages:

i. A comparative analysis within the partner universities with regard to the specific context in which continuing education programmes are offered and their main characteristics and challenges, and taking into account the assessment and assurance of quality in the field of, and/or relevant to, continuing education programmes was conducted.

ii. The design of the overall Framework for QA of continuing education programmes was completed based on the main findings of the analysis report.

iii. A pilot evaluation of a group of continuing education programmes within the partner HEIs was undertaken, using the overall framework and specific tools developed within the project, aimed at examining the operational, organisational aspects and the feasibility of the framework.

The QACEP Project focuses on CEPs that are a subset of all the Life long Learning strategies and Continuing Education activities of HEIs.

Design of QACEP Project
The project stages and activities are briefly outlined below with full details available on the QACEP project web site[6].

---

6   https://www.qacep.eu/Pages/Activities.aspx.

1 - Comparative analysis stage

Step 1 of the Project was to carry out a comparative analysis of the definition and main characteristics of Continuing Education Programmes (CEPs) in each partner institution in order to establish a common understanding of the quality assurance procedures and to identify the main commonalities and differences with regard to quality assurance of CEPs in each.

The analysis was based on a report completed by the six HEIs members of the Consortium. The template for the report had been designed by the Consortium and included specific questions on the topics to be addressed. The completed reports were analysed by one partner and considered at a Workshop in which each partner participated. Based on the written analysis, and the feedback and discussion within the Workshop, a report was drafted and submitted to all partners for comment before finalisation.

2 - Design of the Framework

The principal objective of the Project was to determine the main components of a QA system which addresses the specific needs and issues of CEPs and to design a Framework that can be used by HEIs for QA of CEPs. In designing the QA Framework, the Consortium considered the results of the analysis stage as well as complementary work carried out in this field in other projects. The draft Framework was tested in each of the partner HEIs before finalisation.

3 - Pilot Evaluation

An evaluation of the Framework was conducted in a pilot exercise aimed at verifying the applicability of the theoretical concepts developed in the designed Framework through the testing of specific tools and practical organisational solutions.
The Consortium developed and tested two tools based on the QACEP Framework:

    a. **web-based questionnaire** designed to collect data on some characteristics and features of CEP leavers (learners who had just completed or were about to complete the programme) and their opinions on the learning experience.

    b. **template for a "QACEP Evaluation Report on Continuing Education Programmes".**

Both tools were made available on-line to facilitate ease of use. The choice of CEPs used to test the tools was made by each partner, resulting in heterogeneity in types of programme (in terms of size, credits, length, learning objectives, target groups, etc.). The web platform for the on-line questionnaire was developed by one partner and the results of the survey were made available for the self-evaluation activity.

In each institution selected CEPs were self-evaluated by the programme Managers/Directors with the support of other staff working in the programme. Data was collected directly from participants and a detailed report was generated for each programme according to a specified format.

Project Outcomes & Results
All documents, tools developed and evaluations are available for consideration and use from the QACEP project web site (https://www.qacep.eu/Lists/Outcomes/Outcomes.aspx).

1. QACEP Comparative Analysis: the results and the template model
The comparative analysis focused on common characteristics and relevant differences among the partner institutions with regard to QA of CEPs and good practices with respect to the approaches, working methodologies and specific tools already in place.

The QACEP Comparative Analysis Report, available on the website, was conceived as:

- the necessary basis to design the QA framework for HEIs' CEPs in the next stage of the project;
- a source of examples, with analysis, for dissemination outside the consortium to foster a mutual understanding of contexts, practices and challenges in quality assurance of CEPs at a European level.

The website also contains a paper reporting the results of first phase of the QACEP Project and presented at the European Quality Assurance Forum held in Lyon on the 18-20 of November 2010 (https://www.qacep.eu/Lists/Outcomes/Outcomes.aspx).

The structure of the template reflects the holistic approach to Quality Assurance applied by the Consortium in the project, considering QA of CEPs to be a continuous process (quality cycle) of Planning, Doing, Checking and Acting (improvement).

The questions are structured in six sections, focussing on a distinct issue in each case:

   a. General description of the university/institute (General questions which need to give an idea of the educational national and institutional context as well as the quality assurance context)
   b. Definition and identification of CE within each institution
   c. Identification of planning and set-up procedures for CEPs
   d. Identification of Quality Assurance (QA) procedures for CEPs
   e. SWOT analysis of QA of CEPs
   f. Good practices in QA (of CEPs or other programmes).

<u>Comment:</u> The comparative analysis revealed a great diversity not only in the different types of CE offered in the partner institutions, but even in what are considered as CEPs in the QACEP partners. The analysis revealed many differences in the approach to the internal QA of these programmes, and while commonalities were detected, they were more at the level of underlying concepts and principles. The main areas found in common are:

- The initiative for CEPs is always subject to review and approval by a central body.
- Often there are preparatory steps prior to final central approval, consisting of the evaluation of application forms on the basis of a set of criteria. The common criteria can be grouped in three categories: economic/financial, academic and market related. The design of the programme is always done internally at the university. Involvement of the labour market in evaluations and improvement of the programme is deemed to be crucial.
- Most institutions do have reactive quality assurance procedures in place.

- At a minimum all partner institutions involve the participants/students of the programme in the evaluations and tend to include more or less the same topics in their questionnaires for evaluation.

Partners highlighted the usefulness of the exercise of conducting the comparative analysis in mapping practices and describing the characteristics and processes of their own CEPs and QA systems and the template used for the analysis was deemed to be a useful instrument that can be used by any HEI in the presentation of a general state of the art of its CEPs and the QA system in place.

The format of the template and a summary of the comparative analyses results are available in Appendix A of this Handbook.

2. QACEP Framework

The **QACEP Framework** was conceived as a reference tool for HEIs to strategically manage the quality of its CEPs, by fostering a continuous improvement cycle. The Framework developed by QACEP is generic to guarantee its' usefulness for different types of continuing education providers and it can be used by each individual institution as an aid in developing its own model.

The Framework itself is organised in four parts according to the following phases: Planning and design, Implementation and delivery, Programme monitoring, and Programme improvement.

For each phase the Framework identifies key elements and features deemed to be crucial for a successful programme and so essential for consideration in a QA System for continuing education programmes. The QACEP Framework provides an institutional evaluation tool which can be used by HEIs to self-reflect and evaluate the maturity of their processes.

The QACEP Framework and the toolkit associated with it are described in the following chapters of this Handbook.

QACEP Tools: "Student Evaluation Questionnaire (CEP Leavers Questionnaire)" and "Evaluation report on Continuing Education Programmes"

The Student Evaluation Questionnaire (CEP Leavers Questionnaire), provided in Appendix C, was developed following an in-depth comparative analysis of indicators adopted by partners for similar purposes, and aligned with the QACEP Framework. It includes:

- general information about the learner
- reasons for enrolling in the programme
- assessment on programme organisation, teaching, structures and tools
- assessment on internship/placement experience
- general evaluation of the programme.

The <u>Evaluation Report on Continuing Education Programmes</u>, provided in Appendix B, was developed as a tool to support self-evaluation activities of HEIs' CEPs by reporting in a well organised document the relevant information which is needed to provide informed judgements and to highlight quality factors about the CE programme's aims, teaching and learning methods environment.

During the Pilot the Evaluation Report was provided in an Intranet-based version. The Web Form "simulated" a possible database (or more than one database) where the information about a programme is collected during the lifetime of the programme. Using the intranet tool facilitated the collection of the qualitative and quantitative information for each CEP and the self-evaluation comments into a document (one for each Programme) with a common format.

<u>Comments</u>
The partners found the self-evaluation activity a useful tool to assist in the analysis of the programme and establish weaknesses and possibilities for improvement actions. It provides a useful guide to checking some critical issues/key elements linked with the programme content; useful for compiling the programme infor-

mation made by different units and a base to help the institution in the internal review procedures. It helps programme managers and institutions to clarify what is needed to be achieved; it is useful for both monitoring and reviewing.
Some of the benefits in using the Evaluation Report are that it:
- provides a checklist for design of new CEPs;
- reminds programme managers of aims and objectives;
- provides a common language for discussion across programmes and institution;
- provides a checklist for review of existing CEPs;
- uses a systematic approach and standardizes QA approach;
- provides information and metrics for external stakeholders, especially potential funders;
- highlights areas where attention is needed;
- facilitates programmes planning - irrespective of staff turnover/changes;
- data can be used for publicity purposes e.g. student testimonials;
- facilitates audit procedures, minimizing administration.

Two reports with further details describing the Pilot Stage are available in QACEP website (https://www.qacep.eu/Lists/Outcomes/Outcomes.aspx.)

Why this Handbook?
As a significant part of the dissemination policy of the project this Handbook was published and made available on the project website (www.qacep.eu). It focuses on the principal outcomes of the Project, briefly described above and described in detail in the documents available on the web site.

The aim of this Handbook is to provide support and benchmarking references to HEIs, at the strategic and management levels as well as at the programme level, in the commencement and development of QA systems of continuing education programmes. The Handbook focuses on the main results of the Project and includes the overall Framework for Quality Assurance of Continuing Education Programmes, further fine-tuned after conduct of the pilots. All the basic components of the Framework (programme design, implementation, conformity with specific organisational and resources requirements, monitoring, evaluation, quality improvement) are illustrated by some relevant examples of good practice. The Handbook also provides operational indication and guidelines for organisational/technical solutions.

Chapter 2

The QACEP Framework

"Evaluation is a process that critically examines a program. It involves collecting and analysing information about a programme's activities, characteristics and outcomes. Its purpose is to make judgements about a program, to improve its effectiveness, and/or to inform programming decisions."

Patton 1987

What is the QACEP Quality Framework?

The QACEP Quality Framework is a reference guide for HEIs designed to assist them in the management of the quality of their continuing education programmes, by fostering the development of a continuous improvement approach. The goal is to assist in the development of more efficient ways and means for delivering better outputs with the available inputs.

The target groups for the QACEP Quality Framework are continuing education programme managers, coordinators, teachers/academics, governing bodies and managers of higher education institutions.

Every Higher Education Institution (HEI) can apply the QACEP Quality Framework to their specific needs ensuing from its strategic aims and objectives.

How is the Framework designed?

The QACEP Quality Framework is built on the Plan-Do-Check-Act (PDCA) cycle idea: a problem-solving process to facilitate continuous improvement in organizations. The PDCA concept emphasises that improvement must start with careful planning, lead to effective action, go through monitoring and improvement and re-visit the planning stage again resulting in an improved activity. Therefore, the Framework is organised into four parts, corresponding to the following phases:

- Planning and design
- Implementation and delivery
- Programme monitoring
- Programme improvement.

For each phase the Framework identifies key elements and features. The key elements presented in the planning and design phase must also be considered for all other phases.

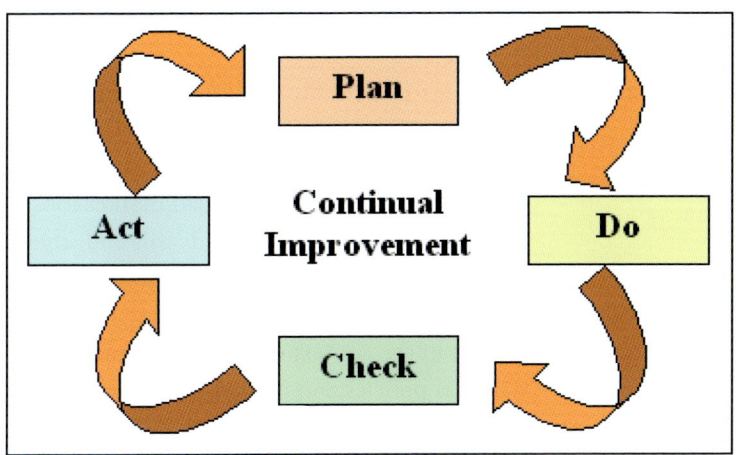

Figure 1. QACEP Quality Framework structure is built on PDCA cycle idea. For each phase the Framework identifies key elements and features.

Key elements and features of the QACEP Framework

Key elements are the features of continuing education programmes that are crucial for a successful performance and so must be considered by any Quality Assurance System for continuing education programmes. They have been developed with due consideration to the Standards and Guidelines for Quality Assurance in the European Higher Education Area (ESG) approved by Ministers for Education in member states who have signed up to the Bologna Process[7].

The Framework includes both key elements at institutional level (such as vision and strategic objectives) and key elements at programme level (such as educational concept and resources).

---

[7]   http://www.enqa.eu/files/ESG_3edition%20(2).pdf

Key Element	Description
Mission, Vision and Values at the institutional level	In order to assure the quality of its continuing education programme offerings, a HEI needs to identify the distinctive features of its offerings, in the context of the broad market for continuing education. Towards this end, the HEI needs to specify its definition of continuing education and the underpinning basic values, in the context of both European and national policies and regulations. The quality of continuing education programmes has to be considered in the context of this definition.
Strategic objectives and management of HEIs	HEIs should identify the specific objectives of continuing education programmes, in the context of the whole range and levels of learning experiences (Certificate, Diploma, Bachelor, Master, doctorate, etc.). It is important that HEIs clearly communicate these objectives to all stakeholders. The quality of continuing education programmes must be considered in the context of these objectives.
Programme design • Target groups	The intended goals of continuing education programmes are tailor-made for specific target groups. Admission criteria and procedures are important in order to ensure an alignment between expected participants/target groups and programmes.
• Programme goals and objectives	The objectives of continuing education programmes should reflect overall institutional goals and strategies and clearly describe the learning outcomes to be achieved by learners.

• Educational concept and structure of the programme	The quality of continuing education programmes should be considered in relation to what extent the structure and educational concept of the programme suits the target group needs (e.g. learning outcomes, length of the programme, study workload, etc.). A clearly defined educational concept in line with strategic objectives and the target group needs is essential to ensure the quality of the programme.
Services	The importance of careful design of the education services provided by a continuing education programme derives from the identification of specific target groups and their needs.
Resources • Personnel	The quality of continuing education programmes depends on the personnel involved in the delivery of the programmes: the teaching staff including both academics and professionals, and other staff including the programme managers, coordinators, administrative support staff, etc. The qualifications, competences, skills and experience of the personnel all contribute to the quality of the programme delivered
• Infrastructure	The infrastructure required to enable the delivery of a successful and high quality continuing education programme needs to be appropriate for the delivery/modes of learning suitable to facilitate the achievement of the programme learning outcomes by the target group.

• Financial resources	Since most continuing education programmes are self-financed, a budget plan detailing anticipated costs and revenues is necessary.

Features

In each phase, the key elements are detailed as features that are suggested actions to be implemented in order to improve the quality factors of the continuing education programmes.

Features of each phase are described in the next chapters.

How is the QACEP Framework toolkit used and/or customizable?

The QACEP Framework in included in a toolkit with the aim of assisting, in a flexible manner, a diverse range of HEIs in the implementation of a quality improvement approach to the design and delivery of continuing education programmes. For example, at the institutional level, the QACEP Framework can be used to support and guide strategies and choices to be taken by the decision makers. At the programme level, the Framework can be used as a programme level check-list to help programme managers to apply these indicators in their work.

The tools developed are provided in Excel format on the QACEP project web site[8], allowing users the possibility of tailoring them to their own specific purposes and to institutional requirements.

The QACEP Quality Framework toolkit consists of the following:
1. **Introduction to the QACEP Framework** describing the principles of the Framework, and how the Framework and its associated tools can be used.
2. **QACEP Framework self-evaluation matrix** for continuing education programme(s) / institutions.
3. **Examples of institutional tools:**
   Tool example 1: Defining stakeholders of the programme for monitoring + tool to help to formulate feedback questions.

---

[8] https://www.qacep.eu/Lists/Outcomes/Outcomes.aspx

Tool example 2: Checklist for evaluation of the quality assurance system.

Self-evaluation matrix tool[9]

The QACEP Framework self-evaluation matrix tool can be used by HEIs to monitor their processes. The matrix requires the institution to score itself with reference to listed features, with the help of a scale description. The matrix tool also allows the description of the roles and responsibilities, procedures, stakeholders involved and the individual tools to be used for each feature.

Institutions may tailor the tool to their specific needs by choosing some of the listed features or by adding new ones. It should be noted that this tool is presented as a guideline matrix and is not inflexible. It can be adapted to suit the needs of individual institutions and programmes.

The tool may be used for describing the roles and responsibilities, the procedures, making notes of the stakeholders involved, and, lastly, listing the tools to be used for quality assurance in the institution.

The tools described here in the first part of the matrix allow the user to review the situation.

Scale descriptor:
Level 1. No processes (Quality depends solely on the individual)
Activities depend on individual initiatives. There are no defined associated assessment processes. Problems are rectified as they arise.

Level 2. Basic processes (Process awakening)
Responsibility for activities ceases to be individual and tends to become a shared responsibility with some short term planning. There is some degree of process definition although there is no documentation. Performance is assessed occasionally.

Level 3. Intermediate processes (Vision through processes, professionalization and a guarantee of quality). There are established standards, procedures and directives

---
[9] https://www.qacep.eu/Lists/Outcomes/Outcomes.aspx

known throughout the organization, unit or service. The activities are carried out in accordance with these procedures.

Level 4. Sophisticated processes (Systematic assessment and improvement of the processes) Established procedures are systematically assessed for potential improvement. The organisation/programme strives to anticipate problems and complaints.

Evidence should be provided for the choice made

FEATURES	Level 1. No processes	Level 2. Basic processes	Level 3. Intermediate processes	Level 4. Sophisticated processes	EVIDENCE
Feature 1					
Feature 2					

The second part (incorporating roles, responsibilities, etc.) is designed to facilitate the user in planning the adoption of tools for the future.

Quality assurance procedure in your organisation

	Roles and Responsibilities	Procedure	Stakeholders involved	Tools used / to be used
Feature 1				
Feature 2				

Examples of institutional tools

The QACEP Framework toolkit provides also two examples of QACEP Organizational Tools. One helps to define stakeholders to be involved in the programme monitoring, and to make specific questionnaires for each group of stakeholders; the other helps to develop a checklist to help staff to implement quality assurance. Other specific tools can be designed by each Higher Education Institution in applying the Framework to their needs. These are available on the QACEP Project web site[10].

---

10 http://www.qacep.eu

Suggestions on how to use and to customize the QACEP Framework

HEIs may use the QACEP Framework at the institutional level as a starting point for brainstorming, internal discussions and as an opportunity for self-reflection, especially because it poses questions and ideas which generate a lot of issues and topics to be discussed. For example:

- It could be used to improve some existing tools, with the highlighting of weaknesses and possible improvements of internal procedures.

- The information contained in the Framework could be used as a basis for discussions with employers and other external stakeholders, facilitating a rethink of strategies and adoption of a general model able to create systems that embed quality within procedures.

- The QACEP Framework provides a standardization of quality policy and standards across institutions, nationally and internationally, together with a tool forming a basis for review.

- The Framework is a driver for quality improvement, providing a common language for design and review.

- The Framework can be used as a checklist, especially helpful for programme directors, who almost always lack time to review and to analyse long documents.

- The Framework can be translated into local languages and the terminology adapted to suit the local situation and traditions.

Chapter 3

Step 1: Planning and Design of Continuing Education Programmes

*" If your vision is for a year plant wheat.
If your vision is for a decade plant trees.
If your vision is for a lifetime plant people."*

ANON

One of the guiding principles in any quality assurance system within higher education (and elsewhere) is to ensure that certain key factors are met. These vary depending on the activity but the over-riding principle is that good planning must take into account certain key elements. One of the principal activities of the project concerned the discussion and development of a checklist of issues which would commonly apply to continuing education programmes. This checklist was developed following the very detailed comparative analysis referred to in earlier chapters of this Handbook. The comparative analysis allowed the partners in the Consortium to base the checklist on existing examples of good practice in institutions across Europe.

It was evident that completion of this checklist and engagement in this type of reflection prior to delivery of a CE programme would ensure that appropriate programmes would be delivered with a demonstrated demand from key stakeholders (learners, labour market) and the necessary resources for delivery available.

Design of Checklist of issues to be considered prior to design and delivery of programme.

In the Table below the key elements, as arrived at in the implementation of this project, are listed and described:

Table: Key elements in planning and design of CE Programmes.

Key element	Feature
Mission, Vision and Values at the institutional level	To what extent is there a mission and vision on the role of continuing education programmes and to what extent do the basic values underpin them within the institution?
	To what extent is there a common vision on the way the institution (as an academic institution) adds value to the continuing education programmes provided?

Strategic objectives and management of the Higher Education Institution		To what extent has the institution defined strategic objectives for delivery of continuing education programmes?
		To what extent is there a strategy on how to interact and communicate with stakeholders on the local, national and international level?
		To what extent does the institution have guidelines with specific criteria included (defining learning outcomes, educational concepts, validation of learning, certification, courses, credits/hours, length of the programme, timetable, study load), on the development of continuing education programmes?
		To what extent is there an approval procedure for continuing education programmes at institutional level?
		To what extent are there clear and communicated criteria for decision-making on whether programmes are allowed to proceed or not?
		To what extent is there a human resources management strategy for continuing education programmes (hiring/appointment, professional development, promotion, etc.)?
		To what extent is there a strategy with regard to the allocation of resources?
		To what extent does the organization align its programmes with the National Qualifications Framework (NQF)?
		To what extent is the process for reviewing programmes transparent?
Programme design	Target groups	To what extent is there a clear process to enable identification of programme target groups and their needs?

		To what extent are the needs of stakeholders (labour market, professional bodies, etc.) assessed?
		To what extent is there a common procedure, at institutional level, for admission of learners? If the institution does not have such a procedure in place, is there a programme specific procedure?
		To what extent are the procedure(s) for admission clearly communicated to the stakeholders?
	Programme goals and objectives	To what extent are the learning outcomes to be achieved by the learner clearly formulated?
		To what extent are the learning outcomes in line with the vision and strategic objectives of the institution?
		To what extent are the defined learning outcomes in line with the needs of target groups and stakeholders (including labour market)?
		To what extent are the learning outcomes in line with the scientific state of the art in the discipline(s) concerned?
		To what extent are the content of the programme and the expected learning outcomes well described to the stakeholders?
	Educational concept and structure of the programme	To what extent are the components of the learning environment in line with the programme goals and objectives and institutional criteria (learning outcomes, assessment of learners, study materials, curriculum, learning activities, etc.)?
		To what extent are the educational concepts of the programme defined (e.g. learner-centred organization of the programme, problem-based learning, on the job training, etc.)?
		To what extent are the programme characteristics (schedule, course materials, teaching methods, etc.) adjusted to the needs of the target group?
		To what extent is the educational concept and structure of the programme clear and transparent to the prospective participants?

Services		To what extent are the support service requirements defined on the basis of the target group needs identified (tutoring, ICT support, guidance, consultation, communication etc.)?
Resources	Personnel	To what extent is the selection of appropriate teaching staff in line with the strategic objectives and educational concepts of the programme?
		To what extent are the competences and skills required of the teaching staff/programme management/director/coordinator clearly defined?

Examples of text used and good practices extracted from the Evaluation Reports on the CEPs in QACEP Pilot

Vision

"Our vision is of a community of scholars which includes all our staff and all our students, a university where effective and imaginative teaching and learning approaches are fostered and supported, where teaching and learning enjoy parity of esteem with research, where a student-centred approach to research-led teaching is embedded in the culture, and where students and teachers enjoy their teaching and learning experiences."

Mission

"In an environment which gives parity of esteem to teaching, learning and research and where students are our highest priority, the University's central roles are to create, preserve, and communicate knowledge and to enhance intellectual, cultural, social and economic life locally, regionally and globally."

Stakeholder Involvement
How are stakeholders involved?

"The planning of the first edition of the programme has been developed by a Scientific Committee and the Association of Industrialists of XXXXXX. Other external stakeholders are invited to give their comments on the programme design."

Specific target-group definition

"This part-time postgraduate course is a University-level programme: a University higher degree (Master) or other higher education certificate is required. Students and alumni typically work for large companies, banks, institutional investors and project development companies, housing companies and centre management firms. They include estate agents, lawyers, town planners, economists, financiers, tax specialists, accountants, engineers, building promoters, project developers, building contractors, architects and, surveyors/valuers."

Stakeholders' needs

"The course was developed after extensive consultation with experts. The curriculum is constantly updated in accordance with market demands and student/teacher feedback. The many specialists involved from both University and professional life guarantee, together with feedback of the students, the outstanding quality, the scientific nature and the practical orientation of the course. This "interaction" proved to be vital for the programme and very relevant to keep a good balance between various components of the course and the real estate sector."

Students' admission

The procedure for selection and admission of students in our Master's and postgraduate courses is:

"Proof of achievement of College (Bachelor / Diploma / Degree)."

"In the case of degrees of uncertain prior learning, the Programme Director will make an assessment of each case taking into account the applicant's career."

Chapter 4

Step 2: Implementation and Delivery of Continuing Education Programmes

"The growth for education and training will be in continuing adult education. Online delivery is the trigger for this growth, but the demand for lifetime education stems from profound changes in society. We live in an economy where knowledge, not buildings and machinery, is the chief resource and where knowledge-workers make up the biggest part of the work force"

Peter Drucker

The QACEP Framework facilitates the careful planning and design of appropriate CE programmes for which there is a good demand from learners and also the labour market, inter alia. It is recommended that the tools and the quality assurance agenda be considered at all stages of delivery of a CE programme.

The QACEP Framework recommends that the main features to be considered in this phase are:

Table:

Feature
To what extent are the main features and characteristics for the successful implementation of the programme defined?
To what extent are the educational concepts and structure of the programme clearly communicated to target groups and other stakeholders?

Successful implementation and delivery of a CE programme is greatly enhanced by not only careful planning prior to the commencement of the programme but also an awareness of the need to continuously review, gather feedback on all aspects of the programme and ensure all teachers understand the need to actively engage the learners in the learning.

Examples of text used and good practices extracted from the Evaluation Reports on the CEPs in QACEP Pilot

Programme Goals and Objectives: General learning outcomes

On successful completion of the programme participants should be able to:
- Recognise the role of personal development and interpersonal skills in management
- Apply business planning tools and techniques to achieve optimal operational and supply chain processes
- Employ best practice project management tools and techniques in operational and supply chain management
- Develop and implement relevant key performance indicators
- Manage- the flow of quality and food safety information across the organisation and along the supply chain to the customer
- Address the complexities inherent in organisation-wide and supply projects and lead Lean SCM teams

Educational Concept and Structure of the Programme
Programme Description

"The programme is structured in two blocks.
The first block comprises modules 1, 2, 3 and 4 corresponds to …..and the second block corresponds to the development of a project by each student. Its duration is 6 months."

How are teaching activities delivered?

"The teaching activities are offered in a traditional way basically through lectures. There is a series of in-class case studies, first hand business presentations from prominent business leaders, business games, and group work assignments in relevant areas, including brand development, logistics and primary purchases, innovation and new product management, innovative marketing strategies."

Students' assessment

"During the course, students are evaluated through a continuous assessment system through the Virtual Classroom (Aula Virtual). After each topic, students take an assessment test of knowledge via on-line. They also do a research project, whose value is taken into account in the final assessment. At the end of the academic year, the students have to take a final in-class exam that takes place in <different locations>."

Self-evaluation of programme design

"The curriculum is constantly updated in line with student and employer demands. To continuously meet the needs of the sector, close co-operation with students, teachers, firms, and partners is believed to be both vital and of outstanding interest for the further development of the programme."

"At the end of a course unit, the students evaluate the program. This evaluation is focussed on the subject matter, teaching methods, the work load, and organisation. This helps us to draw conclusions for the program in the next semester or next year."

SERVICES

Administrative services

"Administrative management for the delivery of the master and the enrolment of students involves:

- Advisory Team: Responsible for information and advice to prospective students and support throughout the process prior to registration.

- Department of Programme Management: Responsible for the coordination of the teaching.

- Department of Community Services: provides additional services, including access to the library and to job platforms.

- Academic Secretary: Responsible for the processing of financial files (payments, validation documentation, issuing of certificates, etc.).

- Platform Department for Design and Production: Responsible for the design and operation of the virtual classroom, as well as design and management of online tests. They also provide technological support to teachers and students."

Placement

"All courses, particularly the part dedicated to practical work activities, are designed to reduce on the-job training time for participants and to offer companies access to well prepared and skilled resources. Placing participants at the heart of a company during the internship period and project work represents the first step in preparing the participants for job opportunities after graduation. Students can choose their traineeship amongst a long list of international firms."

RESOURCES

Personnel

"22 of the 38 lecturers are linked to another University or are professionals representing the profession and chosen among leading individuals in their field. However, several (16, representing 113/221 hours) full time lecturers of the University dedicate a considerable amount of their time to the University programme."

Teaching facilities

"The teaching facilities are: lecture halls, study rooms, libraries, in partner Universities of the network. The students enrolled have the same facilities of all other students enrolled in the University such as discounted rates in canteens, cafeterias, cinemas, theatre, public transportation, sports activities, etc."

ICT learning environment

"Students have the facility to use a reserved area of the dedicated website in order to check class schedule, teaching material, announcements, grades, useful instructions. The website is updated directly by staff."

Chapter 5

Step 3: Monitoring of Continuing Education Programmes

"Evaluating the success of a course entails assessing student learning, so the more explicit faculty can be about identifying evidence of student learning (or its absence) on all dimensions represented in the course goals, the more useful the course evaluation will be."

ANON

A core characteristic of the QACEP Framework is the assurance of the quality of delivery of the programme and the quality of the learning experience for learners. Monitoring of all aspects is essential.

The QACEP Framework recommends that the main features to be considered in this phase are:

Table:

Feature
To what extent is there a procedure to continuously review programmes?
To what extent are the monitoring system and criteria transparent to all stakeholders?
To what extent does programme monitoring include checking the quality assurance of the processes (assessment of learning outcomes, infrastructure, etc.) as well as quality assurance of the quality of achieved learning outcomes?
To what extent are the monitoring procedures well aligned in accordance with programme phases and milestones?
To what extent are the different stakeholders involved in programme monitoring?
To what extent are there defined procedures to collect data and feedback for statistics and reviewing? (E.g. number of participants, learner satisfaction, teaching, infrastructure and services, learning outcomes, etc.)?
To what extent is there a procedure to report the findings of the programme monitoring activities in order to contribute to the strategic objectives and management of the institution? What is the procedure?
To what extent are different stakeholders consulted on the results of monitoring (teachers, learners, companies etc.)?
To what extent is there a process to review the quality assurance procedure of the Higher Education Institution for continuing education programmes?

As a part of the QACEP Project activities a questionnaire to ascertain the views of learners of their learning experience was designed and tested. This questionnaire is given in detail in Appendix C and is also available on-line at the QACEP Project web site (www.qacep.eu). This survey tool is designed to be used on-line, facilitating all learners in participation. During the testing it was also determined that the active engagement of the programme director in encouraging completion of the questionnaire was an advantage. The survey can be customised to suit local needs and can also be translated into an appropriate language.

Examples of text used and good practices extracted from the Evaluation Reports on the CEPs in QACEP Pilot

Internal QA System of the programme

"The Programme has a Quality Assurance System based on anonymous questionnaires for each teaching activity. At the end of the programme, we use the results to give an internal evaluation of the courses/teachers/teaching material, and to plan the didactical activities for the next year. The staff are also involved in the evaluation of new teachers hired for the programme."

Roles and responsibilities

"Each year students can elect a "class president", a representative that can speak on behalf of the entire class, in order to have a direct dialogue in case of particular issues that involve all of the class. The Programme Manager is available to deal with the issues during the semester and provides two dedicated office sessions per week."

Self-evaluation of QA System

"The Programme Manager has created a network on the Internet (Facebook, LinkedIn, Twitter) in which prospective students can meet alumni in order to gain information, tips, suggestions and opinions. We make efforts to have former students engaged, who were positively influenced by the programme, so they can share their feelings with the others."

Employment/careers/importance of internship and companies' agreement in placement

"……….Moreover, a quarter of the interviewees who currently work, have changed their pre-programme occupation, and the remaining three-quarters have started working only after the programme conclusion. Half of this sample think that the programme positively influenced the obtainment of employment, whereas the other half think it has had only a marginal role."

"Feedback for programme design comes from the constitution of a Business Network: partner companies may choose to cooperate with the Programme Staff Team on a medium to long term basis deciding to join this Business Network which provides financial support to selected students and a full set of benefits for the company. …….. The main benefit for companies joining the Business Network is the possibility of offering practical work activities and hiring young managers with international profiles who have a deep knowledge and passion for international business."

Chapter 6

Step 4: Continuous Quality Improvement of Continuing Education Programmes

"Of all our human resources the most precious is the desire to improve"

ANON

Continuous Quality Improvement

In any quality assurance system one of the key features is the improvement that is developed and implemented following the monitoring of the programme including the ascertaining of views of all stakeholders on the delivery and outcomes of the programme.

Key to delivering an improvement and enhancement of programmes is accurate data and evidence on which to base any changes to be made. Thus it is essential that the monitoring phase on the delivery is conducted in a timely and thorough fashion. Self-reflection together with evaluation of the strengths and weaknesses of all aspects of the programme, conducted in an evidence-based manner, will ensure the alignment of the needs of all stakeholders (learners, labour market, teachers, institutions, etc.) and result in delivery of an enhanced programme.

Quality Improvement Plan

A consequence of the self-reflection and evaluation of the programme is the development of a quality improvement plan. The plan should focus on the recommendations for improvement that the programme director is proposing for the future. In developing the plan the writer will be conscious of the plans for improving the quality of the learning experience for students as the central theme. In addition the plans for enhancing the quality of learning of the teaching staff and the supports in place within the institution to deliver this will be developed. There may be changes to the aims and objectives of the programme and in a flexible system, responding rapidly to social and labour market demands, this has always to be considered.

A quality improvement plan will focus on the strategies for implementing the proposals for quality improvement, setting targets that are achievable. A key part of any strategic plan is the operational plan that accompanies it and converts aims and objectives into a set of specific activities, with key performance indicators and benchmarks established. Re-assessment of these on a regular basis will ensure that they continue to be relevant and appropriate in local situations. Measurement of the success in implementing the quality improvement plan (i.e. monitoring) must be both carefully planned and delivered.

In essence this is the core principle of the QACEP Framework. The flexible and customisable tools associated with the Framework were developed with precisely this objective in mind. This was tested in the Pilot phase of the QACEP Project and the Framework was deemed to be sustainable, robust and fit for purpose by the member institutions within the consortium.

The QACEP Framework has defined a number of features for the quality improvement phase as follows:

Table: Continuous quality improvement of CEPs

Feature
To what extent is there a defined process for ensuring the improvement of programmes?
To what extent are the quality improvement system and criteria transparent to all stakeholders?
To what extent is there a procedure to enable the development of quality improvement actions for the programme resulting from the data and information provided from the monitoring system?
To what extent are quality improvement actions discussed with and communicated to internal and external stakeholders?
To what extent are the suggestions/recommendations for improvement reported in a timely fashion in order to allow their prompt/immediate implementation?
To what extent is there a procedure to contribute to the strategic objectives of the institution and their implementation on the basis of the findings?
To what extent is there a procedure for follow-up improvement (training and support for teachers, research, innovative actions (e.g. renewing content, learning activities, support systems, etc.)?
To what extent is there a process to facilitate the improvement of the quality assurance procedures of HEI for continuing education programmes?

Examples of text used and good practices extracted from the Evaluation Reports on the CEPs in QACEP Pilot.

"The program continues to evolve and change in response to comments from local practitioners, students and outside bodies. The key concern is to maintain the quality of the programme and to translate new ideas in a concrete strategic view about the education within the Department."

Communication and Promotion

"The programme is described on a dedicated website, offering "first hand" information to the prospective students. There is a specific section on the website with news, events and media sectors. The programme is published on the official website of the University, and is in the process of registering the copyright of the name and the logo."

"Leaflets, flyers and posters are placed in strategic points such as libraries and study rooms. The programme is often cited as an example of good practice by the University for demonstrating collaboration between companies and the university. "

Describe best practices and opportunities for implementing improvement actions

"Analysing the result of the evaluation questionnaire, it is clear that the classroom used had a negative impact on the students' work. Unfortunately, we faced lots of problems trying to find a suitable space, but we solved these problems by renting a better classroom from another Faculty of the University."

Chapter 7

Looking to the future

"Education is not a preparation for life; education is life itself"

John Dewey

Quality Assurance of Continuing Education Programmes: an on-going process.

Quality Assurance of continuing education programmes offered by higher education programmes is an on-going process that continues throughout the duration of a programme in a formative manner as well as at the end of a programme in a summative exercise. The ultimate aim of any quality assurance exercise must be the improvement and enhancement of a programme/activity and it is important that all stakeholders - students, staff and external stakeholders – are facilitated in their engagement with the process. Funding agencies, including government and industry, where applicable, also play an important role in the quality assurance and have an interest in the outcomes and developments.

The economic, political and social environments that we live in today are continuously changing and it is very necessary that all programmes, but especially continuing education programmes, offered by HEIs can respond to the needs of society in a dynamic and flexible manner. An appropriate quality assurance system, which is primarily aimed at improvement, will assist and facilitate all providers of CEPs in the development and delivery of suitable and appropriate programmes with maximum benefit to the learner.

Bologna Process

The Bologna Process, endorsed and adopted by 47 countries in Europe, places the learner and the learner's needs at the centre of higher education. To assist countries in focussing on the role of higher education institutions in facilitating learning and offering a quality experience to learners ten action lines were developed from the principles of the Bologna Framework. Principal among these is quality assurance and in the stocktaking and follow-up exercises that have been conducted on a regular basis over the past number of years, the effectiveness of the implementation of quality assurance procedures developed within countries and institutions is paramount. It is notable that, as we continuously work to improve the systems, there is an ever-increasing focus on quality improvement and quality enhancement as a key outcome of quality assurance processes.

QA is a key element of the Bologna Process and, since the main responsibility for quality lies within HEIs, it is important that they should continue to develop their systems of QA, and not neglect their commitment to assuring the quality of their CEPs with the same rigour and professionalism as they assure and improve the quality of mainstream undergraduate and postgraduate programmes.

One of the guiding principles of the Bologna Process is the facilitation and encouragement of transnational mobility of both students and staff. Linked to this is the facilitation of mobility of graduates.

The field of advanced continuing education offered by HEIs lies at the intersection between university and general vocational continuing education and training. To support transparency of information, comparability and a correct co-location in National Qualification Frameworks, Quality Assurance systems are required to support the adequacy of the evidence to be provided on educational programme design and on the learning outcomes to be achieved.

By experimenting in a transnational perspective, and by validating, in well-chosen pilot trials, innovative tools and methodologies for the QA of HEI's CEPs, the QACEP Project aims to support the process of innovation that is leading European HEIs to become "lifelong learning centres". In the pursuit of this aim, HEIs are defining new strategies aimed at opening up a wider range of top quality educational services to new learners and to returning learners. It is hoped that the Project results will stimulate raising awareness on continuing education among HEIs as a major contribution to the wider agenda on lifelong learning.

The labour market currently calls for new skills and new jobs: it requires appropriate infrastructures for continuing education and training of adults to prevent forms of generational discrimination into employment policies: even well specialised and graduate professionals are required to improve personal skills and competences. HEIs have a responsibility to bring coherence and quality to this type of learning offering to create opportunities for retraining and/or advanced specialisation for all.

Advanced knowledge-based societies require innovative and creative educational systems able to respond swiftly to the specific needs of the labour market and able to provide research-based learning, training and retraining. In the pursuit of this aim, HEIs must define articulated strategies for lifelong learning and find ways to open up educational services to returning learners.

Conclusion

The QACEP Project has aimed to contribute to the on-going debate on quality assurance and quality improvement of higher education and all its associated programmes, with a particular focus on CE. However the tools are also adaptable to all programmes and it is hoped that institutions will be able to maximise the benefits from use of the tools.

Appendix A

QACEP Comparative Analysis template

Note: *This Comparative Analysis Template can be used by HEIs to present a general state of the art with respect to its CEPs and the QA system in place. During the QACEP Project this template was developed and then completed by each partner institution and the results from each were compared.*

The items addressed within the QACEP Comparative analysis template included a general introduction to the university/institute, the identification of continuing education within the institution and the definition of continuing education programmes, the identification of procedures with regard to the design of the CEPs, the identification of quality assessment procedures, a SWOT analysis and finally the description of some good practices. The template is based on the concept of the quality cycle (PDCA). In this way concentration was focused on the phases in which CEPs are designed (plan), in which they are implemented (do), in which the monitoring and evaluation of CEPs take place (check) and the actions that are taken in order to improve programmes (act).

The plan phase of the quality cycle refers to the process before the programme is running (= ex ante). For the identification of planning and set-up procedures, attention was paid to initiative, decision, design, promotion and marketing and support. The check and act phases of the quality cycle include actions that are taken once the programme is running (= in itinere) as well as when the programme has ended (= ex-post).

The template and the final comparative analysis are available on the QACEP project web site (https://www.qacep.eu/Lists/Outcomes/Outcomes.aspx).

Name of your institution:
This questionnaire has been completed by:

    Name: Function:

1. **General description of the university / institute.**
    1.1 Describe the educational context/system of your university, e.g. which programmes you organise, what is the context in the broad offer of

education (national, regional, …)?

1.2 Describe the quality assurance system in your university / institute in a general way, as well as the philosophy behind this system.

1.3 Is there a legal framework for quality assurance? Explain.

2. Identification of continuing education within the university / institute.

2.1 Describe the Life Long Learning strategy at your university.

2.2 Give your definition of 'continuing education'. In order to clarify the definition, it is also useful to describe explicitly what it is not.

2.3 Is there a legal framework concerning continuing education in your country and/or region? If yes, please explain.

2.4 Describe the regulation of continuing education within your institution.

2.5 Describe the current role of continuing education in your country and institution

2.6 Describe the local context/market of continuing education.

2.7 Describe the future role of continuing education in your country and institution

2.8 In general how is the funding of continuing education organised in your institution?

2.9 What are the different types of continuing education your institution offers? Is there a structure/classification of these types? If yes, please describe the criteria for this structure/classification.

2.10 Describe the characteristics of these different types of continuing education (CE).

	Type 1 of CE	Type 2 of CE	Type 3 of CE	...
Size*				
Certification*				
Admission requirements*				
Target group				
Funding*				
Credits*				
Exam regulations				
Quality Assurance				
Number of specific different activities per type of CE				

* Mandatory fields

2.11   What percentage (estimation) of these programmes is organised:
- through only distance education (online or e-learning)?
- explain your interpretation of distance education
- through only traditional education (classroom education)?
- through a combination of distance and traditional education (blended)?

2.12   What percentage (estimation) of these programmes is organised:
- for minimum Bachelor's degree?
- for minimum Master's degree?
- no qualification necessary?

2.13   What percentage (estimation) of these programmes is organised:
- in evening and/or weekend classes?
- in a company or in a professional environment (i.e. outside university)?

- in the institute/university?

2.14 In which study domain or faculty lies the focus of continuing education? Which study areas have a rather small offering of continuing education? Explain, if possible.

	study domain or faculty	study domain or faculty	study domain or faculty	...	Total
Type of CE					
Number of students					
Type of CE					
Number of students					
Type of CE					
Number of students					
Total number of CE					
Total number of students					

2.15 What is the share of students participating in continuing education in relation to the total number of students?

2.16 Give your definition of 'continuing education programmes'. In order to clarify the definition, it is also useful to describe explicitly what is not considered continuing education.

3. **Identification of planning and set-up procedures for <u>continuing education programmes</u> (programme management).**

3.1 With regard to the initiative to organise a continuing education programme:
    3.1.1 Who takes the initiative (idea) of offering a continuing education programme?
    3.1.2 How do you determine the need?
    3.1.3 Which institutional unit(s), stakeholders (both internal and external) or other persons determine the target group, the conditions, the curriculum, etc.?
    3.1.4 How do you monitor the reasons for opting for a continuing education programme (as opposed to something else, e.g. Master)?

3.2 With regard to the **decision** to organise a continuing education programme:
    3.2.1 Which institutional unit(s), (internal and external) stakeholders or other persons are involved in the decision as to whether or not an idea for continuing education programme will be implemented?
        3.2.1.1 *At which level the decision is taken?*
        3.2.1.2 *Are there specific procedures that the decision makers need to respect?*
        3.2.1.3 *Is there a formal approval?*
    3.2.2 Is there a procedure to be followed in order to organise a continuing education programme? Define the responsibilities. Provide examples of the documents that are required.
        3.2.2.1 *Is there an application form to be completed?*
        3.2.2.2 *What are the main subjects / different elements in this report / these documents?*
        3.2.2.3 *Are these documents (report) being evaluated and/or approved? By whom and on which terms / conditions / criteria?*

3.3 With regard to the **design** of a continuing education programme:
    3.3.1 Who is responsible for the concrete design of the programme?
    3.3.2 How is the academic level and the involvement of the professional field assured during the entire process?

        3.3.2.1 *How do you define academic level?*
        3.3.2.2 *How do you monitor the academic level?*
        3.3.2.3 *Who is responsible for the selection of students of the programmes and how is this organised?*
        3.3.2.4 *How is prior learning involved in continuing education programmes?*
        3.3.2.5 *How are students evaluated?*
        3.3.2.6 *How do you involve the professional field in the process? For example as stakeholders, teachers, work placement (stage), hosts, …?*
        3.3.2.7 *How do you monitor 'involvement of the professional field'?*

3.4   About the **promotion and marketing** of a continuing education programme:
        3.4.1 Who is responsible for the promotion of the programmes and how is this organised?
        3.4.2 How is fundraising organised inside and outside the university?

3.5   About the **support** in the planning and set-up of a continuing education programme:
        3.5.1 Do the organisers of continuing education programmes have any kind of support from other institutional units, departments, services or external institutions? How is this organised?

4. Identification of quality assessment procedures for continuing education programmes (quality management).

Part 4 does not ask for the evaluation of one particular programme, but is more generally about evaluation procedures for continuing education programmes.

4.1   Who or which official body/authority is responsible for the quality (management) of the continuing education programme? What are their main responsibilities?

4.2   Which stakeholders are structurally involved in the quality management?

4.3   Are the continuing education programmes being evaluated

(internally and/or externally)? Please explain the quality assessment procedures. Make a clear distinction between internal and external procedures if applicable.
- 4.3.1 Who is responsible for the evaluation? Who takes the initiative?
- 4.3.2 Which topics are addressed in the evaluation?
- 4.3.3 Which stakeholders (incl. participants) are being questioned in the evaluation?
- 4.3.4 How often are they evaluated?
- 4.3.5 Is there a follow-up to the evaluation? How is this organised and by whom?

5. SWOT analysis of quality assurance of continuing education programmes.

- 5.1 What are the strengths and weaknesses of the quality assurance approach with regard to continuing education programmes within your institution?
- 5.2 What are the main opportunities and threats your institute is facing concerning quality assurance of continuing education programmes?

6. Good practices of quality assurance.

- 6.1 Define one or two specific examples of good practice in quality assurance (of continuing education programmes or something else that could be applicable).
Define the approach, the work methodologies and specific tools. Provide examples of the documents.

Example of the use of the of Template for comparative purposes: summary of the comparative analysis for QACEP Partners.

A **common definition of "CEPs"** was achieved using the following elements:
- **Programmes are organised and certified by the university itself.** This also implies for example the use of logos, uniform certification, etc. There may be

other initiatives or programmes where members of staff may be involved, but they stand outside university, are certified in a different way and their overall quality falls outside the university's responsibility.

- **Size and credits (two aspects of the same characteristic)** are important, in that a minimum critical size is required for a continuing education activity to be considered a "programme". Most universities define such a minimum. Rather than just a minimum in size, the fact that participants make a certain progression during the programme is considered to be a characteristic of CEPs. **Thus a CEP usually consists of several identifiable parts.**

In addition, two more characteristics stand out and were discussed in more detail: the **academic level** and the **involvement of the professional field.**

Plan phase – Within QACEP partners the initiative for CEPs can be taken by a very wide range of persons or units within the university or institution, but is always 'channelled' through internal units. The need for a programme is determined by both central and non-central (meaning at university or at LLL centre level) bodies or a mixture of both. There are many different ways, from needs analysis, market research and surveys, etc. to determine internal motives.

The institutional units involved range from central services to programme committees and individual professors, but these initiatives are always subject to review and approval by a central body. Since all institutions also offer regular (bachelor and master) programmes, they all have ways of monitoring whether or not the choice for continuing education is the best way to realize the intended goals. Reaching a common set of criteria may not be possible, but it is important that each institution has its own explicit criteria.

The decision to organize a CEP is always taken by a central unit or person. Often, but not always, there are preparatory steps prior to the final formal approval, which always involves a specific procedure in one form or another, at the institutional level. This procedure, consisting of several steps and requiring specific documents, is widely considered to be a key element in quality assurance. Common criteria for the evaluation of these forms could be grouped into three main categories: economic/financial, academic and market related. The importance of some of these criteria is specific for CEPs, compared to other programmes.

The design of the programme is always done internally at the university, even if the idea or initiative comes from outside – though external partners can and will participate. The academic level is crucial and all partners agree that there should be a definition at least at each institution. The degree and nature of involvement of the professional field in designing the programme is very wide: as stakeholders, as representatives from the professional field, etc., as members of committees responsible for the programme, in organizing internships/placement and, finally, as teachers when appropriate. Monitoring of the involvement of the professional field is usually done centrally as part of the approval procedure. Once the programme is organised, monitoring is conducted more usually at programme level, making it more difficult.

Promotion and marketing are organized in the broader context of the institution's communication scheme; support can be drawn from internal units or can be external.

Check and act phases (once the programme is running as well as when the programme has ended) - With regard to the official bodies or authorities engaged in the quality management of the programmes and their specific focus of responsibilities, a distinction can be made between the responsibility for the overall quality and daily management of the programme, for the quality of the individual course, for the definition of QA procedures and policy decisions in the field of QA and finally for the administration and implementation of QA procedures and of evaluations. Depending on the internal organisation of the institution, these responsibilities are attributed to one or more official bodies/authorities, either at the local (programme) and/or the central (institutional) level.

Hence a typology was identified for quality management or QA structures related to the type of institutions involved in the project. Thus, in some institutions, responsibility for both the definition of QA procedures as well as the organisation of evaluations and for the overall quality and daily management is situated at faculty and programme level. These universities have a more or less decentralised organisation when it comes to CEPs.

At other institutions, however, the definition of QA procedures and policy, as well as the organisation of evaluations, are taken care of by separate central units of the university. The involvement of academic staff and faculties in quality assurance of the CEPs is restricted to the daily management of the programme. Thus, in these institutions, the official body responsible for the definition of quality assurance procedures/policy and for the organisation of evaluations is different from that responsible for the daily management and quality of the CEPs.

Other institutions have systems that are situated in between both types, as some general QA procedures for some types of CEPs may be identified centrally, whereas some individual programmes may still have a large degree of responsibility and autonomy.

A distinction may also be made between more substantial CEPs, which often have a formalized management structure and to a certain degree are regulated by central policy, and CEPs of a rather small size which are often under the responsibility of one (academic) individual and often "escape" any type of policy or rules. The same distinction counts for more or less permanent programmes vs. single, occasional or cyclical programmes.

It was concluded that the way in which these responsibilities are defined, depending on the internal organisation of the institution, is of no/minor importance. What matters is that responsibilities and accountability are clear for each area of operation in order to have an adequate management process. When it comes to the involvement of (internal and external) stakeholders in the quality management of CEPs, it seemed that there was no common denominator: many different stakeholders - in changing composition - are involved. Thus, programme committees usually contain academics, and in some cases also students. External stakeholders, i.e. labour market or customer representatives, are represented in external advisory boards, which also include teachers (academics and non-academics). Labour market representatives tend to have an important role in providing advice on the content of the programme in order to adapt the programme content to special (labour market) needs and changing contexts.

CEPs are not involved in external (i.e. external to the institution) QA procedures, as none of the programmes needs to obtain an official recognition and accreditation by the government. As for the internal quality assessment of CEPs, some institutions have standard procedures in place, clearly defined in documents or manuals. Most are reactive QA procedures as they focus on the quality of the programme that was delivered and take place at the end of the course, module or programme (evaluation by students after the course, by alumni, feedback by the labour market on the effectiveness of the course, etc.).

All partners involve the participants of the programmes in the evaluations. Some also include other stakeholders, such as teachers and employees of labour market representatives. Especially for CEPs, the involvement of the labour market in evaluations is deemed crucial.

Apart from questionnaires, feedback discussions amongst staff, students, employers or within an external advisory board are usual. The evaluation by students concerns both individual courses and the entire programme. Basically, four main groups of topics in questionnaires can be detected in every institution: teacher/teaching activities, coherence and content of the programme, professional orientation, organisation and infrastructure.

When it comes to the follow-up phase, evaluation results must be taken into account by both individual teachers and programme direction for updating the framework, skeleton and main lines of the programme and/or the courses. In some institutions, evaluation results are reported at the institutional level and used as input for the central policy. Sometimes, bad results can lead to the decision to remove a programme from the institution's suite of CEP's.

Further suggestions on how to use and customize the "QACEP Comparative analysis template"

- HEIs can use the template internally as a first brainstorming and the basis to review procedures;
- HEIs con use the list of questions as a guide to describe and present to other Institutions their organisation concerning Continuing Education and Quality Assurance.
- The comparative table, in the first part of the template, can be used to compare the characteristics of CEPs within a wide group of institutions avoiding the problem of the different use of terminology that can arise.

Appendix B

QACEP Evaluation Report for Continuing Education Programmes

Note:

As described in Chapter 1 of this Handbook the **"Evaluation Report on Continuing Education Programmes"** *was developed as a tool to support self-evaluation activities of HEIs' CEPs. The self-evaluation is conducted by considering a list of key elements identified as crucial for the successful performance of a CEP and that should be considered for its QA.*

For each section (Programme Design, Services, Resources, QA System, Communication, Promotion, Figures) the Evaluation Report should be completed with specific information about the programme in order to provide evidence on how the programme has been planned, implemented and monitored. The information reported should be the contents produced and the results obtained at different times during the life of the programme:

- *during the planning phase of the programme (identification of target groups, admission of students, programme goals, etc....)*
- *during the implementation of the programme (timetable of activities, infrastructural supports, etc....)*
- *during the monitoring activities (no. of applicants, no. of enrolled students, students' opinion, etc...).*

The self-evaluation fields, located at the end of each section, require an analysis of the main strengths and weaknesses of all aspects of the programme. Through this self-analysis every programme should highlight its best practices (considering its main strengths), and should plan improvement actions (considering its weaknesses). Some guideline questions are provided in order to help the analysis.

This form and the report on the self-evaluations conducted during the pilot exercise can be downloaded from the QACEP web site (https://www.qacep.eu/Lists/Outcomes/Outcomes.aspx).

PROGRAMME OVERVIEW
General information about the programme.

Institution vision and mission
Description of the vision and mission of the Higher Education Institution about its Continuing Education Programmes, in the context of the demand for continuing education.

Description of the type of programme qualification, according to the National Qualifications Framework.

Title of the Continuing Education Programme:

Manager / Director /Coordinator:

Department / Faculty /Institute:

Year:

PROGRAMME DESIGN
Information in this section describes:
- *how the programme goals and learning objectives have been developed*
- *how the different components of the programme have been designed and implemented*
- *how the overall organisation has been tailor-made to the educational concept and target groups*

I. Stakeholders involved
The design of a Continuing Education Programme requires an effective interaction with internal and external stakeholders.

- **Stakeholders involved in planning the programme**
   Identify the stakeholders involved in programme design and

organisation (faculty, department, professors, employers, local community, etc.).

- **How are stakeholders involved**
  Describe the procedures used to involve stakeholders.

II. Target Groups

The intended goals of Continuing Education Programmes are tailor-made for specific target groups and should answer the needs of specific stakeholders.

- **Specific target-group definition**

Describe the specific target groups for the programme. (Examples: undergraduates, first-time employees, professionals, managers, unemployed, specialised technicians, etc.).

- **Stakeholders' needs**

Identify the need of stakeholders as resulting from labour market analysis, consultation of employers, professional associations, credit union associations, local associations, etc. Describe how the programme specifically meets these needs.

- **Admission of Students**

Describe the procedures and criteria for selection and admission of students (admission requirements, entry test, qualifications, etc.)

IV Programme Goals and Objectives

The objectives of Continuing Education Programmes should describe the related professional profiles and the intended learning outcomes to be achieved by learners.

- **Professional profiles**

Describe the professional profiles/additional professional competences

- **Expected learning outcomes**

Describe the expected learning outcomes in terms of knowledge and understanding,

V Educational Concept and Structure of the Programme

The structure and educational concept of the programme should meet the target group needs. A clearly defined educational concept, in line with programme goals and objectives and the need of the target group, is essential for the quality of the programme.

- **Programme description**
General description of the structure of the Programme. (Summary)
- **Length of the Programme**
Describe the length of the programme in terms of hours, ECTS, years, hour/ECTS.
- **List of subjects/modules**
List of the subjects/modules and their learning outcomes.
- **How are teaching activities delivered**
Describe teaching activities organisation (traditional, e-learning, blended learning, etc.).
- **Programme organisation**
Describe the programme organisation (terms, period for assessment, traineeship, timetable, etc.).
- **Assessment of Students**
Describe the methods adopted for the assessment of students (continuous assessment, examinations, final dissertation, internship assessment, etc.)
- **Other teaching activity not mentioned before**

VI   Other aspects deemed relevant to the programme design section.

Self-evaluation of programme design

Comment on the information reported in the section "Programme design" emphasizing main strengths and weaknesses. In writing the comment take into consideration features such as:

To what extent:

- are the needs of stakeholders assessed?
- is the process to identify programme target groups, and their needs, efficient?
- the learning outcomes to be achieved are clearly formulated?
- are the contents of the programme in line with the scientific state of the art in the discipline(s) concerned?
- are the components of the learning environment in line with the programme goals and objectives and institutional criteria?

- *are the programme characteristics (schedule, course materials, teaching methods, etc) adjusted to the needs of the target group?*

In the commentary make reference also to the figures available in section 6. For example:
1. *students' opinion*
2. *no. of applicants*
3. *no. of participants*

Describe best practices and opportunities for implementing improvement actions.

SERVICES

Information in this section describes how the design of the support services provided takes into consideration the programme organisation and the specific needs of the target groups.

Administrative services
Describe the administrative and support offices (student affairs office; student admission office, etc). Describe how students enrol, how student records are kept and maintained and how student transcripts are delivered.

Tutoring and guidance
- **Tutoring**
  Describe the role of the tutor and how and when he/she can help students to carry on their studies.
- **Guidance**
  Describe the guidance service and how and when it can help students before, during and after programme attendance and in relation to professional roles.

Placement
  Describe placement services and their relation with companies and labour market.

Other facilities
  Describe other facilities for students (accommodation office, catering, health care, etc.).

Self-evaluation of services
Comment on the information reported in the section "Services" emphasizing main

strengths and weaknesses. In writing the comment take into consideration the following:

- *to what extent are the support service requirements defined on the basis of the target group needs identified (tutoring, IC support, guidance, consultation, communication, etc.)?*

In the commentary make reference also to the figures available in section 6. For example: students' opinion on services.

Describe best practices and opportunities for implementing improvement actions

RESOURCES
Personnel
The personnel involved in Continuing Education Programmes are teaching staff, including both academics and external professionals, and other staff including the programme managers, coordinators, administrative support staff, etc. The qualifications, competences, skills and experience of the personnel all contribute to the quality of the programme delivered.

- **Teaching staff**

  List the teachers. Specify if they are academic professors or external professionals. Indicate the qualification, the field of study and the part of the programme they are responsible for.

- **Programme Support staff**

  Specify the number of support and administrative people involved in the programme and if they are full-time or part-time. Describe the different roles and services provided.

Teaching facilities
The infrastructure required to deliver a successful and high quality Continuing Education Programme needs to be appropriate for the achievement of the programme learning outcomes by the target groups.

- **Teaching facilities**

  Describe the teaching facilities (infrastructure) used in the Continuing

Education Programme.
- **ICT learning environment**
Describe ICT learning environment required for the Continuing Education Programme.

Financial resources
Financial resources necessary for the delivery and the implementation of the continuing education programme.
- **Student fees**
Describe the procedure to define fees. Description of the method of payment.
- **Scholarship/Grants/ Funding opportunities**
Describe the availability and the procedures for students to apply for scholarships, external grants or funding provided by employers /EU /national or local government and the procedures to apply for them.

Other aspects deemed relevant for the Resources section.

Self-evaluation of resources
Comment on the information reported in the section Resources emphasizing main strengths and weaknesses. In the commentary take into consideration the following guide questions:
- to what extent is the selection of appropriate teaching staff in line with the strategic objectives and educational concepts of the programme?
- to what extent are the competences and skills required of the teaching staff/programme management /director /coordinator clearly defined?

In writing the comment make reference also to the figures available in section 6. For example: students' opinion on resources.

Describe best practices and opportunities for implementing improvement actions.

QUALITY ASSURANCE SYSTEM
The Internal Quality Assurance System of the continuing education pro-

gramme should provide transparency, accountability, correct delivery of the designed programme, monitoring activities and appropriate improvement reactions.

Internal Quality Assurance System of the programme
Describe Quality Assurance procedures adopted at programme level.
Roles and responsibilities
Describe the well-defined roles and responsibilities for each person or committee involved in the Programme.
Other aspects deemed relevant for the Quality Assurance section.

Self-evaluation of Quality Assurance System
Comment on the information reported in this section emphasizing main strengths and weaknesses. In the commentary take into consideration features such as:

- *to what extent are the roles and responsibilities of all personnel involved in the programme planning, implementation, monitoring and improvement clear and in line with the competences needed to deliver the programme?*
- *to what extent are the monitoring procedures well aligned in accordance with programme phases and milestones?*
- *to what extent are the different stakeholders involved in programme monitoring?*
- *Describe best practices and opportunities for implementing improvement actions.*

COMMUNICATION
This section describes the communication strategy aimed to correctly inform and to promote the Continuing Education programmes to external stakeholders.

Methods/tools
Describe how the programme is communicated to external stakeholders (what kind of information is delivered e.g.: list of teachers? learning outcomes? ...) and by means of which tools and procedures (website, newsletter, marketing plan, etc.). Indicate staff/ committees/ institutions involved in communication (programme manager, companies, etc.).

Other
Other aspects deemed relevant for the Communication section.

Self-evaluation of communication and promotion
Comment on the information reported in this section emphasizing main strengths and weaknesses. In writing the comment take into consideration the following features:

- *to what extent are the learning outcomes to be achieved clearly formulated?*
- *to what extent are the content of the programme and the expected learning outcomes well described to the stakeholders?*
- *to what extent are the educational concept and structure of the programme clear and transparent to the prospective participants?*
- *to what extent are the educational concepts and structure of the programme clearly communicated to target groups and other stakeholders?*
- *to what extent are the monitoring system and criteria transparent to all stakeholders?*
- *Describe best practices and opportunities for implementing improvement actions.*

FIGURES (Statistics) FOR THE PROGRAMME
Figures (statistics) for the continuing education programme.

I. No. of applicants
Figures should refer to a specific year of reference. A chronological trend of the previous editions is welcomed. This field concerns only programmes in which admission procedures are required.

II. No. of students enrolled
Figures should refer to a specific year of reference. A chronological trend of the previous editions is welcomed.

III. No. application /students' quota
Figures should refer to a specific year of reference. A chronological trend of the previous editions is welcomed. This field concerns only programmes in which admission procedures are required.

IV.　No. of students enrolled /students quota

Figures should refer to a specific year of reference. A chronological trend of the previous editions is welcomed.

V.　No. of students who successfully complete the study programme

Figures should refer to a specific year of reference. A chronological trend of the previous editions is welcomed.

VI.　No. of students who attend learning activities

Identification of a quota of attendance coherent with the programme. Indication of the n. of students reaching the established quota. Figures should refer to a specific year of reference. A chronological trend of the previous editions is welcomed.

VII.　Final grading (average)

Indication of the average grade of the students attending the programme, and, where applicable, trend of the previous editions is welcomed.

VIII.　Students' opinion

Results of QACEP Survey on student's opinions.

IX.　Employment /careers/ importance of internship and companies agreement in placement

Institutional data on employability, if applicable.

X.　Teachers' opinion

Institutional data on teachers' opinion, if applicable.

XI.　Other stakeholders' opinion (companies/labour market)

Institutional data on other stakeholders' opinion, if applicable.

XII.　Other

Any other additional figures available useful for self-evaluation.

Further suggestions on how to use and customize the Evaluation Report on CEPs

- **Customisation of the list of information required by the Evaluation Report:** the suggested list is very comprehensive in order to facilitate self-reflection, but it is possible to simplify the list of information required and to avoid duplicated information. It is of course also possible to add additional areas as required by an institution – for example selection procedures for teachers, additional support services, etc. Each institution should also adapt the vocabulary to the own context and define the data required. Institutions will have different objectives and the template should be customised to reflect this.

    In many instances it would be useful to include a final overall SWOT analysis of every element.

- **Support for Self-Evaluation of Continuing Education Programmes:** It is important to offer all the support and help required to programme managers and to highlight the benefits of this work and to persuade them that this is not just additional work but a service benefitting both the programme and the institution.

    The benefits of using the web form and an integrated approach to the collection and analysis of data means that work does not have to be repeated and that the database of all information required to evaluate the programme is pre-existing at the time of the self-evaluation exercise.

Appendix C

QACEP Student Evaluation Questionnaire (CEP Leavers Questionnaire)

Note: *This questionnaire was developed during the QACEP Project and the list of questions derived from an in-depth comparative analysis of indicators adopted by partners for similar purposes, and aligned with the QACEP Framework. Main topics are:*

- *general information about the learner;*
- *reasons for enrolment in the programme;*
- *assessment on programme organisation, teaching, structures and tools;*
- *assessment on internship/placement experience;*
- *general evaluation.*

The questionnaire was administered to the participants in the 22 CEPs through an online platform.

This form and the report on the Pilot self-evaluation can be downloaded from the QACEP Project web site at https://www.qacep.eu/Lists/Outcomes/Outcomes.aspx.

A. GENERAL INFORMATION
1. Age
2. Where did you live immediately before taking part in the programme?

Same region/community/county of the attended programme; other region/community/county but same country; other EU country; other European country (extra-EU); Africa; Asia; North America; South and Central America; Oceania

3. Which is the highest qualification that you had/were about to attain at the time of enrolment in the programme?

Bachelor; Master; PhD; other postgraduate qualification (specify); other (specify)

4. Where did you achieve the highest qualification that you had at the time of enrolment in the programme?

Name of the institution (specify)

5. What kind of job position did you hold during the programme?

Full time job; Part-time job; Occasional, Fixed term or seasonal work activities; none

6. How did you finance your participation in this programme?

Scholarship/Grant; Self-finance; Employers; other (specify)

7. How did you get to know about the programme?

Through the web site of the university; Through other web sites; Through email advertisement; Through an advertisement seen in the newspapers; Through a leaflet advertising all the university's programmes; A teacher or another staff member of the university told me about the programme; People who had previously attended this programme told me about it; People who have not attended this programme told me about it; other (specify)

Answer the following questions (section B, C and D, except open questions 24, 25 and 35) with a score ranging from 1 to 6; 1 = strongly disagree; 2 = disagree; 3 = somewhat/rather disagree; 4 = somewhat/rather agree; 5 = agree; 6 = strongly agree

B. REASONS FOR PROGRAMME ENROLMENT
The following factors influenced my decision to enroll in the programme:
8. Opportunity to pursue personal interest
9. Prospect of facilitating career improvement
10. Opportunity to acquire professional skills
11. Prospect of facilitating immediate access to the labour market

C. EVALUATION OF PROGRAMME, ORGANIZATION, FACILITIES, TOOLS, , ETC.

12. The objectives/learning outcomes of the programme were clearly stated beforehand
13. The acquired theoretical background was in line with the objectives/learning outcomes of the programme
14. The acquired practical/professional skills were in line with the objectives/learning outcomes of the programme
15. The programme is well-structured (consistent as a whole, no overlaps, no gaps,..)
16. The topics of this programme were thoroughly explained by the teachers
17. Enough time was dedicated to practical activities.
18. Enough time and activities were dedicated to peer-learning from other participants
19. The teaching material (course materials, guidelines, etc.) were satisfactory for study
20. The activities carried out during the internship/traineeship were satisfactory and relevant to the programme
(Skip question if the programme did not feature an internship/traineeship)
21. The administrative services related to the programme were satisfactory
22. The schedule (days of the week and hours of instruction/training) was satisfactory
23. The classrooms were satisfactory
24. The equipment for the teaching activities (projectors, blackboards, computers, laboratory equipment, etc.) was satisfactory
25. The laboratories and/or libraries were satisfactory?
26. Was there a part of the programme with which you were particularly satisfied? If so, which one(s)? [open question]
27. Was there a part of the programme with which you were particularly dissatisfied? If so, which one(s)? [open question]

D. OVERALL PROGRAMME EVALUATION

28. I was satisfied with the programme overall
29. I was satisfied with the teachers/lecturers

30. I was satisfied with the overall learning experience (e.g., I have acquired new competences or updated concepts)
31. The contents of the programme meet my expectations
32. This programme may facilitate my access to the labour market or improve my professional status
33. I would recommend this programme to others
34. The fee for this programme corresponds with the quality level of the activities carried out
35. Please give your suggestions for improving the programme or add a comment about your experience. [open question].

Further suggestions on how to use and customize the Questionnaire and organize a survey about CEPs participants.

- The list of general information required could be modified/integrated considering that the main objective is to put in relation how some "groups" of leavers answered the questions (are there any difference according to the "age", "employment condition"….?).

- Customize the list of questions considering whether:

    a) the main aim is to benchmark results achieved by different CEPs in an established group of programmes and context (one should be careful when applying it given the diversity, for example, of target groups and reasons for participation).

    b) the main aim is to get feedback on a single CEP (in this case more open / qualitative answers could be necessary);

    c) the aim is both to benchmark results and to get feedback on a single CEP (in this case it could be useful to organise the questionnaire in two parts).

    Whether the survey is conducted using an on-line or a paper-based system it is important to explain to learners the aim and importance of the survey. For example, in order to achieve a satisfactory response rate in an online survey a well-designed "invitation letter" is a key success factor.

- This is an example of a questionnaire orientated to evaluation / customer satisfaction. Other useful results for the quality improvement of CEPs could be obtained by submitting to participants a questionnaire focused on "learning reflection".

Appendix D

QACEP Consortium Partner Profiles

The following is a brief description of the partner institutions involved in the project. Full details are available on the individual institutional web sites.

University of Bologna (www.unibo.it) (Lead Partner)

The University of Bologna (UNIBO) is one of the most important institutions of higher education across Europe with more than 80,000 enrolled students, 23 faculties, 69 departments and 3,200 academics. UNIBO has adopted a multi-campus structure and is today one of the most internationalised of all the Italian universities. UNIBO offers more than 200 degree programmes (bachelor and master), PhD and postgraduate vocational training programmes, which offer the opportunity of obtaining a qualification certifying the competencies acquired, and the official recognition of university credits. To promote Quality Assurance of learning programmes according to European Standards and Guidelines is one of the strategic priorities of UNIBO.

University College Cork (www.ucc.ie)

University College Cork (UCC), founded in 1845, is a collegiate university with a long tradition of excellence in research and teaching. The high quality education provided, enriched by a distinctive university experience, is sustained by demand from highly qualified applicants from diverse social and cultural backgrounds. The University is outward looking, and actively engaged in a range of innovative developments in research, teaching and learning. The University has 18,000 students, with approximately 2,500 learners pursuing adult education/distance education/continuing education/professional development programmes ranging from certificates to degrees. The University has four Colleges and provides higher education qualifications in almost all disciplines.

University of Warsaw (www.uw.edu.pl)

The University of Warsaw (UW), founded in 1816, is one of Poland's largest (53,696 students in 2010) and finest universities. It offers 37 major fields and over 100 specializations in the Humanities and Earth, Social and Natural Sciences. All UW fields have the accreditation of the State Accreditation Committee (fields: Biology, Mathematics, Informatics and Economics were awarded outstanding ratings). The University of Warsaw offers postgraduate studies and e-learning studies (The Centre of Open Multimedia Education – COME). The part of UW structure is also the Open University.

Aalto University (www.aalto.fi)
Aalto University, established in 2010, was created from the merger of three Finnish universities: The Helsinki School of Economics, Helsinki University of Technology and The University of Art and Design Helsinki. The six schools of Aalto University are all leading and renowned institutions in their respective fields and in their own right. Aalto University Professional Development (Aalto PRO) offers a wide range of open university courses, continuing education programmes and development services for companies, public bodies and individuals. Lifelong professional development ventures offer preparedness to respond to the needs of today's working life, and its expertise in foreseeing technological and economic prospects is used to help customers secure their future.

Katholieke Universiteit Leuven (www.kuleuven.be)
K.U.Leuven, founded in 1425, is Belgium's largest university. As a leading European research university, it offers a wide variety of academic programmes in Dutch and English, nurtured by high-quality interdisciplinary research, both at the University and at its internationally acclaimed University hospitals. Over 6,000 researchers from over 120 countries participate in curiosity-driven and strategic frontier research, as well as targeted and demand-driven research. As a comprehensive university, K.U.Leuven offers 3-year Bachelor's and 1 or 2-year Master's programmes in almost all disciplines. The Leuven doctoral schools organise the international PhD tracks of close to 4,000 doctoral students.

Institute for Lifelong Learning, University of Barcelona (www.il3.ub.edu)
Institute for Lifelong Learning (IL3-UB) is a Foundation created by the University of Barcelona with the aim of promoting an education attractive to students at all stages in life. IL3-UB has been established from two initiatives of the University of Barcelona: Les Heures and the University of Barcelona Virtual. IL3-UB's mission is to provide the training programmes to students and companies needed to achieve

their goal for personal and professional development. IL3-UB shares with the University of Barcelona a solid base of research and qualified teachers. From this base, scientific findings and the knowledge accumulated through professional experience are easily transferred to the students.

Inter-University Consortium AlmaLaurea (www.almalaurea.net)
AlmaLaurea Inter-University Consortium was established in Italy in 1994 to provide services to graduates, universities and companies. It provides reliable and updated documentation useful to government bodies for policy making decisions on higher education. AlmaLaurea gives feedback to Universities on teaching quality and about graduates' features and job conditions. AlmaLaurea represents approximately 78% of annual graduates, from 64 universities out of 77 in Italy. AlmaLaurea manages a huge database of graduates' CVs, (1,550,000) published both in Italian and English. 150,000 CVs are added to the databank yearly and are updated by the graduates themselves. The AlmaLaurea experience can be defined as a success story.

Coimbra Group (www.coimbra-group.eu)
Founded in 1985 and formally constituted by Charter in 1987, the Coimbra Group is an association of long established European multidisciplinary universities of high international standard committed to creating special academic and cultural ties in order to promote, for the benefit of its members, internationalisation, academic collaboration, excellence in learning and research, and service to society. The Coimbra Group aims to influence European education policy and to develop best practice through the mutual exchange of experience. The Coimbra Group has developed fully fledged Erasmus Programme activities, facilitates student and staff mobility, and participates in EU-funded projects within the framework of e-learning and virtual mobility.

Bibliography

Bologna Process, *Ministerial Declarations and Communiqué*

    (2009) Leuven/Louvain-la-Neuve Communiqué

    (2007) London Communiquè

Davies, P., (2007) *The Bologna Process and University Lifelong Learning: the State of Play and Future Direction.* EUCEN, Barcelona.

(full report: http://www.eucen.eu/BeFlex/FinalReports/BeFlexFullReportPD.pdf)

European Commission Erasmus LLL programme –

http://ec.europa.eu/education/lifelong-learning-programme/doc78_en.htm

European Universities Association – http://www.eua.be/Home.aspx

European Universities Association (2008) European Universities' Charter on Lifelong Learning. EUA, Brussels.

European Universities Continuing Education Network - http://www.eucen.eu/

QACEP Project - https://www.qacep.eu/

Trends reports - www.eua.be/Publications.aspx

Trends I:

Haug, G. and Kirstein, J. (1999) Trends in Learning Structures in Higher Education.

Trends II:

Haug, G. and Tauch, C. (2001) Towards the European higher education area - survey of main reforms from Bologna to Prague.

Trends III:

Reichert, S. and Tauch, C. (2003) Progress towards the European Higher Education Area.

Trends IV:

Reichert, S. and Tauch, C. (2005) European Universities Implementing Bologna.

Trends IV:

Reichert, S. and Tauch, C. (2005) European Universities Implementing Bologna.

Trends V:

Crosier, D., Purser, L. and Smidt, H. (2007) Universities shaping the European Higher Education Area.

Trends VII:

Sursock, A. and Smidt, H. (2010) A decade of change in European Higher Education.

Partners Websites:

University of Bologna - www.unibo.it

University College Cork - www.ucc.ie

University of Warsaw - www.uw.edu.pl

Aalto University - http://www.aalto.fi/en/

Katholieke Universiteit Leuven - www.kuleuven.be

Institute for Lifelong Learning, University of Barcelona - www.il3.ub.edu

Inter-University Consortium AlmaLaurea - www.almalaurea.net

Coimbra Group - www.coimbra-group.eu